Library of Congress Cataloging-in-Publication Data Available

10 9 8 7 6 5 4 3 2 1

An Imagine Book
Published by Charlesbridge
85 Main Street
Watertown, MA 02472
617-926-0329
http://www.charlesbridge.com
Text and Illustrations © 2011 by National Fire Protection Association
Sparky is a trademark of the NFPA

For more information about Sparky, visit www.sparky.org

For information about custom editions, special sales, premium and
corporate purchases, please contact Charlesbridge Publishing, Inc.
at specialsales@charlesbridge.com

ISBN 978-1-936140-62-6

Printed in China
Manufactured in July, 2011

SPARKY™
THE FIRE DOG

Written by Don Hoffman
Illustrated by Todd Dakins

www.sparky.org

Sparky is a trademark of the NFPA

imagine!
Publishing

Welcome to Fire Station Number 5, everyone! My name is Sparky. I'm the good-looking fire dog sitting down in front. Dogs like me that have white fur with black spots are called Dalmatians.

I'm an important member of the Fire Station team.
I help wash and wax the fire truck, and straighten the hoses.
I love the fire station. But I didn't always live here.

I used to live outside a schoolyard. Every day a nice girl fed me pieces of her peanut butter and jelly sandwich.

One day I followed the girl home from school. Suddenly I smelled smoke. Her house was on fire! I ran all the way to the fire station to tell the firefighters.

The firefighters put on their gear and went to work putting out the fire. The little girl and her family were saved. I was a hero!

The firefighters took me back to the fire station and made me part of their team. When the fire alarm sounds, we all jump into the truck. I sit up front, next to the captain. At night, I dream that I am a superhero: Sparky the Fire Dog!

"Look, it's Sparky the Fire Dog!"
Roger Rhino cries, pointing to the sky.

"Hi, Sparky," says Ellie Elephant. "What are you doing here?"
"Do you want to play Frisbee with us?" asks Iggy Iguana.
"I'm looking for fire dangers. And I need some Junior Inspectors to help me." "We'll help!" Roger, Ellie, and Iggy shout.

Roger knocks at Mrs. Sheep's front door.
"Hello! I'm out baaaack," a voice calls.
"It's Sparky and the Junior Inspectors.
We're here to inspect your smoke alarms."

Mrs. Sheep lets us in and I change the battery in her smoke alarm. It's important to test the battery every month to make sure it's working. Mrs. Sheep thanks us and gives us the mittens she's been knitting as a reward for our help.

Mr. Alligator opens the door, and I see a fire in the fireplace and a plugged-in space heater. "It's dangerous to sleep with a fire going," I tell him. "And you should make sure your space heaters are far away from curtains and furniture." "Thanks, Sparky," Mr. Alligator says. "I'll remember that next time."

Mrs. Flamingo is in her front yard next door.

"Hello, Mrs. Flamingo," I say. "Is that a candle I see burning inside your house?"

"Oh, yes. I love the smell of candles."

"Did you know that candles can tip over and start fires? They're nice when you're around, but it's safer to blow them out when you can't pay attention to them." "I never thought of that," says Mrs. Flamingo. "Thanks for the tip, Sparky. I'll be more careful."

Next Ellie brings the Junior Inspectors to her home.

"Ellie tells me you have an escape plan in case of a fire," I say to Mrs. Elephant.

Mrs. Elephant nods and shows us the plan.

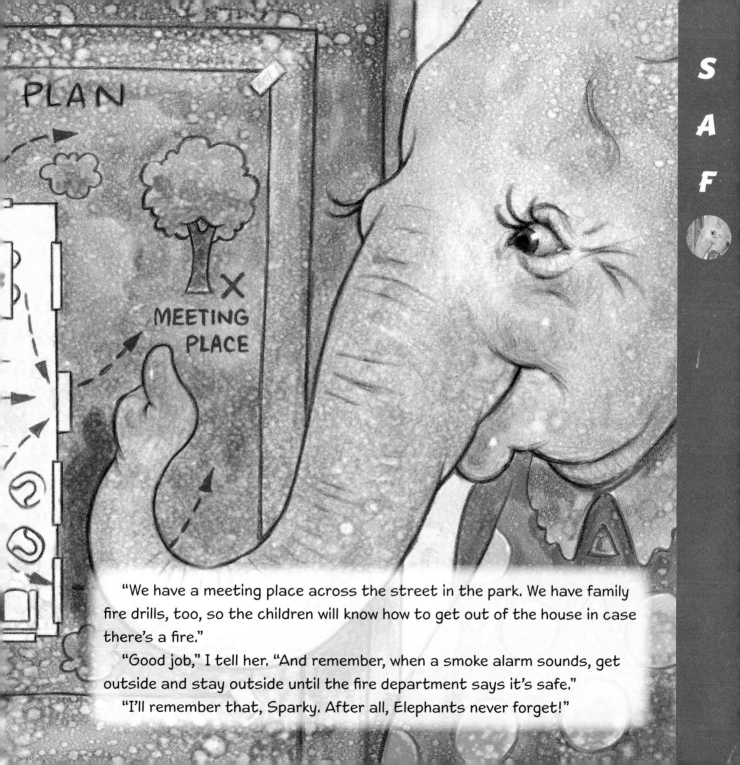

PLAN

MEETING PLACE

"We have a meeting place across the street in the park. We have family fire drills, too, so the children will know how to get out of the house in case there's a fire."

"Good job," I tell her. "And remember, when a smoke alarm sounds, get outside and stay outside until the fire department says it's safe."

"I'll remember that, Sparky. After all, Elephants never forget!"

The **T**iger family lives at the next house.

"Hi, Mrs. Tiger. I'm Sparky the Fire Dog. I see you have twins. They must keep you busy!"

"They sure do. Especially when I'm cooking," Mrs. Tiger says.

"We can help with that."

The Junior Inspectors measure out a safety zone around the stove. "A three-foot 'kids-free' zone around the stove and anything else that gets hot will keep your little tigers safe," I say.

"Thanks for all the help, Sparky."
Something smells yummy at Mrs. Yak's house.
"Come in, come in. I'm making blackberry jam," Mrs. Yak calls.
"Be careful, Junior Inspectors!" I caution. "This pot is very
hot. It's a good thing the handle is turned away from the edge
of the stove."

Our next stop is the Fox house.
"We're making changes in our bedroom,"
Grandma Fox tells us. "Come in and see."

"It's very woodsy," I say. "I see you have two ways out—the door and the window."

"Yes, you never know when you might have to get out of the den quickly."

"That's very sly of you, Grandma Fox."

"I want you to meet my grandpa," Iggy says, pulling all of us along to his house.

When we get inside, I see that Mr. Iguana has left matches and a lighter on the table.

"You should keep matches and lighters up high in a locked cabinet—out of the reach of children," I tell Mr. Iguana. "And Junior Inspectors, if you find matches or a lighter, tell a grown-up."

"I want to be a firefighter just like you when I grow up," Iggy says.

Our next stop is Roger's house.

"Hi, Mrs. **R**hinoceros. I'm here to ask you a few questions about fire safety. Do you know who to call if there is an emergency?"

"That's easy—the fire department."

"Do you know the number?" I ask.

"I know! I know!" exclaims Roger. "It's 9-1-1."
"Good for you, Roger. You got it right!"
"Thanks for stopping by, Sparky," Mrs. Rhinoceros replies. "Come back and see us any time."

"Mmmm, I smell barbeque!" I say as we continue down the street.

"Yes, I'm grilling my famous fish burgers," says Mr. **S**eal.

"It looks like the little seals are playing too close to your grill. They could get hurt. And remember, never use the barbeque grill indoors."

"Right on!" Mr. Seal shouts. "Fish burgers for everyone!"

CLANG!
CLANG!

When we finish our burgers, we move on to the next house. Mrs. Turkey answers the door.

"Hi! My name is Sparky the Fire Dog. I noticed that you don't have a number on your house. It's important for firefighters to be able to see your house number from the street. That way they can find your house quickly in case of an emergency."

"Thanks, Sparky. We'll fix it right away."

"C'mon, Junior Inspectors. It's time to go. I think I hear an alarm."

"Right on!" Mr. Seal shouts. "Fish burgers for everyone!"

CLANG!
CLANG!

When we finish our burgers, we move on to the next house. Mrs. Turkey answers the door.

"Hi! My name is Sparky the Fire Dog. I noticed that you don't have a number on your house. It's important for firefighters to be able to see your house number from the street. That way they can find your house quickly in case of an emergency."

"Thanks, Sparky. We'll fix it right away."

"C'mon, Junior Inspectors. It's time to go. I think I hear an alarm."

I wake up with a start. The fire alarm is ringing!
I jump into the fire truck, right next to the captain,
and the truck races to a fire. I love being a fire dog!

Sheep · Alligator · Flamingo · Elephant · Tiger · Yak

Fox · Iguana · Rhinoceros · Seal · Turkey

Did you notice that the first letter of each animal name spells **SAFETY FIRST**? Safety is very important.

Sparky's Safety Tips

1. Make sure your home has working smoke alarms on every level and inside every bedroom. A grown-up should test all the smoke alarms at least once a month.

2. When you hear a smoke alarm go off, get outside and stay outside.

3. Decide on a place outside where everyone should meet. Practice your escape drill with your family at least twice a year.

4. Know two ways out of the house. In case of a fire, go to your meeting place immediately.

5. Know how to call the fire department after you're outside.

6. Space heaters should be at least three feet away from anything that can burn. Turn heaters off when you leave the room or go to bed.

7. Make sure grown-ups blow out candles when they leave the room or go to bed.

8. Matches and lighters need to be kept up high, in a locked cabinet. If you find matches or a lighter, tell a grown-up.

9. Stay out of the "kids-free zone" when grown-ups are cooking. (The "kids-free zone" is a three-foot space around a stove or outside grill.)

10. Check that your house number can be seen from the street during the day and at night.